Kibbles for the Soul

Poems About the Joy, Irony, Fatalism and Transience of Life

Fifth Edition
Draft #21 POD

Kibble Defined...

The word is pronounced: ˈki-bəl with two syllables.

In this book I adhere to the first meaning listed below. The other definitions or usages have been found on various Internet pages.

1. Pet snack or food, used as munchies or treats in between meals.

3. British dictionaries state that Kibbles began in reference to bucket used in mining.

4. *Kibbles and Cocktails* is the name of a benefit fund raiser held for rescue dogs.

Kibbles for the Soul

©.Kimeldorf.2017

SearchInc Press, Tumwater, WA
Martin Kimeldorf reserves all copyrights for his personal writing and his PhotoArt work. This excludes the quatrains reprinted from *Rubáiyát of Omar Khayyám* in the introduction *Here's Woofing At You.*

No part of this book may be re-sold, shared, reproduced, stored in a retrieval system, or transmitted in any form or by any means electronic or mechanical, including but not limited to: photocopying, recording, or otherwise, without written permission from the author. For permission, write

Dedication

This book is dedicated to ALL my favorite companions. It begins with Judy and Franky (living with me), plus the memory of all my dogs who came before: Pan, Kurly, Micky, Mitzy, and Jack.

Micky Memorial

Table of Intents

Here's Woofing At You...	6
Family, Laughter, and Serving...............................	21
Doubting Religion and Endless Study	37
Epicurean Fatalism	43
Topical Poems	49
Howling In Changing Times	67
Play2Work2Play	78
Celebrating Love...	93
The Paradoxes In Our Aging	100
Chasing Life's Shadow Show	106
The Star Dusty Sky	112
Draining The Cup	116

HERE'S WOOFING AT YOU

Franky Performs for Kibbles

In *Kibbles for the Soul* I set before you a table of my favorite poetic and photographic treats or kibbles. You are invited to nibble on my beloved quatrains (poems) and enjoy the images capturing special moments in the lives of my adored companions. The story I'm about to unwrap is flavored by my blues harmonica, pet photography, and continuous questioning. My kibbles have evolved out of a life-long reading and recitation of the poetry found in the *Rubáiyát of Omar Khayyám.*

In both Persian and British cultures, poetry has been revered as art and entertainment. Persians enjoyed memorizing and reciting verses at social gatherings and in meetings. The short ruba'i (verse) was an ideal form for these oral exchanges. Since Khayyam left behind no poems written in his own hand, it has fallen to others to record his poems. Around 1460, a little over 300 years after Omar's death, the scribe Mahmud Herbudaki, recorded his poetry in Shiraz, Persia.

Some 400 years after the Shiraz manuscript appeared, the Victorian nonconformist Edward FitzGerald fell in the love with the collection. He described how reading the poetry was like looking into a mirror and seeing himself. FitzGerald gave the poetry wings in 1859 when he translated it into English, using the well-loved iambic pentameter form popularized by John Milton and Shakespeare.

Pursuing a skeptical and poetic vision had not always been easy for Omar Khayyám and Edward FitzGerald. According to experts, Persians kept their spirit of independence alive while Grecian, Turkish and Arabic invaders attempted to dominate their culture. Persian poet-rebels spoke out against the early Muslim pieties and the mullahs' attempts to stamp out their native Zoroastrian religion.

Born into wealth in the 1800s, Edward FitzGerald also rebelled against his society's Victorian hypocrisy and self-righteous piety. His acquaintances would describe their loyal friend with words like *bohemian* or *unorthodox*. Eventually both poets would come under attack by the small-minded fundamentalist and demagogic elites.

Together, these two freethinkers formed a cross-cultural and literary *partnership* spanning more than 700 years and two continents. FitzGerald referred to this collaboration as a *FitzOmar* way of life. FitzGerald's version of the poem went on to become the most translated, illustrated, quoted, and recited poem in the world.

In 2017 I wrote about the grand FitzOmar artistic connection, and my experiences with the poetry, in a booklet titled *Sipping From The Rubáiyát's Chalice*. A few of my own quatrains snuck into that work. *Kibbles for the Soul* includes these earlier poems and the many that followed. This is my homage to their vision.

Sharing a Rebellious Heart and Paying the Price

The freethinking, skeptical poets Omar Khayyám and Edward FitzGerald shared a rebellious spirit. Like the Greek skeptics and epicurean philosophers, the FitzOmar crew doubted the existence of an afterlife. They both rejected the existence of heaven and hell. The poets refused to succumb to the fear of death while they lived. Khayyám and Fitzgerald preferred to make the most of the years they had been given; to enjoy the simple pleasures of each day— living by the Latin phrase *carpe diem*—seize the day! Their freethinking ways extended to personal choices about romance, drink, dress and conventional roles.

Unfortunately religious fundamentalists have a long record of persecuting or destroying skeptics, doubters and freethinkers from the realms of science, religion, and art. After Omar's royal benefactor and protector was assassinated, he had to leave his observatory and city, retire to a farm, and outwardly perform as a devout Muslim to save his neck. Since FitzGerald's greatest popularity came after he died he faced a lesser danger. Still, in the 1920s and 1930s, FitzGerald and his poetry would be attacked by puritanical prohibitionists, Nazis, and various religious extremists.

Christian and Moslem fundamentalists often accused the two poets of being self-indulgent, epicurean hedonists or "drinker-thinkers." But after looking at the facts of their lives, we find these accusations remain powerless before the beauty of their words and the historical record.

In fact the ancient Greek originators of skeptical and epicurean philosophy were by no means hedonistic. Socrates conducted classes barefoot to emphasize the value of the simple and contemplative life. Later his fellow truth-seeker, Epicurus also rejected the materialistic lifestyle—avoiding gourmet gluttony by eating the same simple food each day. Epicurus had the radical notion of admitting women and slaves as well as free men into his classrooms. Both Socrates and Epicurus shunned wealth, power, and fame—both refused to charge fees for teaching. The truth is that both the Greek philosopher Epicurus and FitzGerald believed in moderation, and rejected excessive or chronic intoxication and eroticism.

The long-standing battle between inquiry versus faith, between the spirit of reason and the spirit of suspicion, continues into the present moment. In the East we find self-proclaimed true-believers trying to rebuild an exclusionary Muslim caliphate, while in the West their Christian counterparts try to turn a secular America into a nation-state organized around the Bible rather than the Constitution. My first quatrain expresses my concerns over the current religious extremists who quote their holy books to stir up fear and justify vengeance, hatred, and violence.

I

Warmongers sending bomb and gunboat
With God on their side—did each one quote.
The Bible, Talmud, Koran snuff out the light
Fundamentalists justify, then scapegoat.

Critical Thinking Begins With Doubt

The FitzOmar team valued learning and curiosity unrestrained by convention and crude dogma. They both spent a life doubting religious and intellectual orthodoxies. Their rebellious streak dances within the lines of the next FitzOmar quatrain.

Since neither truth nor certitude is at hand
Do not waste your life in doubt for a fairyland
O let us not refuse the goblet of wine
For, sober or drunk, in ignorance we stand

Kibbles for the Soul

Franky's Doubting Peek-a-Boo

While Omar Khayyám and Edward FitzGerald were keenly aware of the joy of learning, they also recognized its inevitable limits. They both knew that study alone could not provide all the answers. Khayyám's poetry, at times, seems dialed in to his fellow Sufi's mystical notions about the universe, while FitzGerald incorporated various transcendental, even magical, phrases into some of his quatrains. Together they wisely laid out the limits of the rational mind in the following lines:

The desire for knowledge, I could not forego
Few secrets remained that I did not know
For seventy-two years, I thought night and day
Until I came to know, I had nothing to show.

For many of us, science and study are essential starting points. And, regardless of one's education, everyone can experience a sense of awe before the starry mystery of our universe. Our doubt or wonder leaves room for appreciating the mystical or intuitive road to understanding. Perhaps these shared feelings can become a bridge between science and religion.

Franky Reaches His Limits of Learning

A Shared Path for Science and Spirit

Khayyám and FitzGerald believed that death closes a final door on our individual stories. But I have departed from this belief as I pursued the *Rubáiyát* questions: *Where do we come from? Where do we go?* I found a middle ground between the FitzOmar-Greek philosophies and those who feel that death is not an absolute end in itself.

My search for an answer began after my father died in 1983. Following his passing, I set out on a 25-year research project investigating the possibility that life renews itself. My inquiry focused on finding a meaning within and beyond my father's death.

My father Don was a respected scientist, lover of poetry and art; a thoughtful, humorous, and wise person—always trying to help his sons grow into fulfilled adults. He taught us a lot about biology and physics, photography and folk music, and civil rights. I learned that the first law of thermodynamics meant that matter could NOT be created, nor destroyed. Therefore, I refused to believe that my father's energy-spirit was completely gone after he passed on.

While the FitzOmar duo believed that the "The flower that once has blown forever dies," I found that notion a bit wasteful. First of all, old rose petals can nourish new growth—adding back in nutrients and possibly suggesting a direction or blueprint for the next bud. Eventually I gravitated toward my unique understanding of how rebirth follows death, as if following a cosmic code.

In my initial research, I noticed that cosmologists were surprised to discover that many of their laws or mathematical descriptions possessed a perfect inter-relatedness. For example, various formulae describing gravity, the expansion of the universe, or anti-matter are defined by their exponents. And if any exponent had varied by a part of one digit, then life never could have begun and planets would have never been born. A mystical beauty surrounds these interlocking formulas; a beauty not reducible to scientific reasoning alone. Just as spiritual leaders insist our lives are governed by moral codes of conduct, scientists similarly demonstrate how codes of a different kind direct the behavior of matter itself.

My research, intuition, and poetry began to lead me toward a general understanding of how a unifying cosmic code might guide the properties of matter, human thinking, evolution, and the vast cosmos itself. The humanist and scientist Albert Einstein phrased it a bit differently when he wrote: the *universe is not random*. The notion of a coded or orderly universe belongs to the mystic and the scientist alike. Later I would write a quatrain summing up my thoughts as follows:

II

Matter neither created nor destroyed, we're told.
I sense the Stars recycle our cosmic code
The eternal truths Reincarnated:
Birth into death into rebirth, all flows…

Kibbles Keeps Me Humble

For me, dogs are one of our greatest gifts. Dogs are among my best and most enduring friends. They live reliably in the present moment no matter how the circumstances change. When the horizon grows bleak or blurry, my best friends urge me to go for a walk. My dogs woof into my soul. They redirect my gaze towards a new vista; one offering hope and possibilities. This experience is captured a bit in my favorite FitzOmar quatrain:

Ah Love! could thou and I with Fate conspire

To grasp this sorry Scheme of Things entire,

Would not we shatter it to bits — and then
Re-mould it nearer to the Heart's Desire.

My first award in photography came from entering pictures of my Franky in an Oregon Humane Society photo contest. He treats my soul with kindness and understanding and humor. I return the favor by treating him with kibbles. My dogs (and my wife Judy) are all the companions I need in this life.

The Three Puppy Frankys

Next, I want to share with you some of my most recent treats. I do not think of them as great poems, but rather as tiny kibbles for the soul. And that thought keeps me centered in the present with my dog and wife. Thinking in terms of kibbles also keeps me humble and laughing. This is why I have chosen to illustrate this small collection of verse mainly with pictures of dogs.

Kibbles for the Soul

Martin and Jack, we yack

Welcome to FitzOmarDorf Poetry

In this book, like my previous one *Sipping From The Rubaiyiat's Chalice,* I have chosen to organize quatrains under various thematic headings. It is useful to point out that a given chapter heading or subheading theme is a subjective construct. Thus, many poems can easily have more than one theme and fit in more than one chapter.

In keeping with Edward FitzGerald's *Rubáiyát of Omar Khayyám* tradition, I number each poem with a Roman Numeral. FitzGerald's first edition contained 75 numbered poems. Later in subsequent editions he changed the number of poems and the numbering scheme for the poems began to break down over time in future editions.

When I reached 77 poems for this book I chose to keep the number associated with a given quatrain fixed. New poems have been subsequently numbered but then placed in what I felt was the best position in this book without attempting to re-number all the poems. This is why you will see poems numbered 78 and above seemingly out of order in regard to their nearby quatrains.

I view my poems as inspired by the spirit of the *FitzOmar way of life*. My versifying efforts are cast in everyday language and include contemporary jargon and even slang. The poems cover traditional topics like youth, learning, irony, love, doubt, aging, fate, and happiness. The kibbles also speak to current themes centered on technology, careers, cosmology, climate change, apocalypse, and politics. Hopefully my effort extends in some small way the FitzOmar's poetic, ironic, and accepting worldview.

In our present darkening medieval moment, hopelessness is easily spawned. For me the counterweight begins when I embrace the epicurean fatalism espoused by the versifiers. The poets urge us to seize happiness in the present moment, rather than delaying or waiting for a future that may never come. And when you finish the last page in this book, I hope you will fill your wine cup with joy and laughter rather than pessimism and fear.

FAMILY, LAUGHTER, AND SERVING

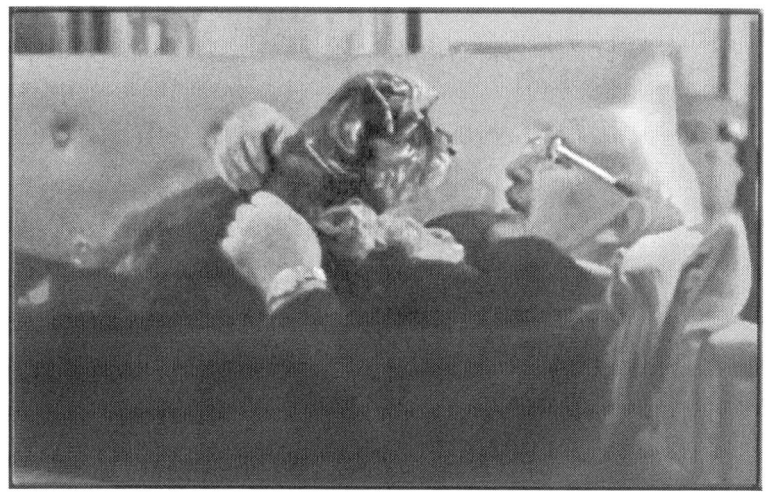

After Heart Surgery, Micky Comforts My Father Don

The great cycle of family-making-traditions often begins with storytelling; hopefully sprinkled with laughter and learning along the way. These quatrains begin with stories about my family and spread out to envelope the power of humor. This chapter also tries to underscore the power we gather when serving others. The Reverend Dr. Martin Luther King said it best when he stated with deep conviction: "Everyone can be great, because everyone can serve."

My Family Story...

III

We anted-up Ideas, words valued as aces,
Language pounded the table, pasted grins on faces.
Debate and laughter, sprinkled like salt and pepper.
Conversations flung us into faraway places...

Bill and Jerry, circa 1917

IV

Their looks, poses, greetings—always mine.
My most devoted friends, forever canine!
Stroking their soft coat soothes my anxious heart,
I taught them tricks—my furry Einsteins.

Judy and our Furry Einstein

LXXXV

Mother's Day or Father's Day, Birth of days…
Time slips away, taking us too long to say,
"You've made me ready for the world."
Forever cherishing how I was raised.

Laughing and Serving Others

My fatalistic stew is always made with a pinch ironic humor. In the midst of dark moments I remind myself to pause and recall how my best-laid plans only make God laugh. I smirk and murmur beneath my breath, "no good deed goes unpunished." Mocking my condition with ironic sayings soothes difficult moments. Pain dissolves when I gleefully yowl at the follies or the absurdities surrounding me.

Laughter has often been prescribed as a healing tonic: we laugh to survive. This is why I consciously seek out moments filled with mirth and playfulness. This might include watching an old favorite comedy, having tea or engaging in make-believe with children, and ignoring the doctor while enjoying a glass of wine. The chuckling helps me regain my footing and perspective.

Serving others also helps me stop focusing on MY pain or problems. This can include working in a soup kitchen, taking a neighbor to a doctor, or phoning a lonely friend. Whenever I put time into helping others, it sweetens my daily cup. Adding doses of humor and service strengthens my ability to recuperate and bounce back after adversity.

V

My half Empty cup brought me a frown,
then I shared some with the transient in town.
Strange how emptying my glass filled and blessed
me with the kindness of a royal crown.

CXVII

What kind of dream fits in a Mercedes Benz?
Mansions, yachts can't feed the soul in the end.
Spirit sprouts from heroic and poetic deeds.
No one turns gold into true, lasting friends

Jack and Judy Share A Moment

VI

**Thoughts too serious means too many pills.
Then I learned to laugh to survive my ills.
Shadows still fall, yet I remain upright,
as laughter heals without the doctor's bill.**

Kibbles for the Soul

VII

**There's no cure for being born human,
marked by pain and later within…
Tease yourself to survive your Self.
Laugh first and avoid ending broken.**

Lifelong Quest for Kibble

LXXX

**Defined by only our aches and our stains?
Or do we enjoy the life that remains?
The riddle is not so easy to unlock,
there's no clear path for the sinners or saints.**

Pooch Café by cartoonist Paul Gilligan

LXXXIII

**I choose to live in a gingerbread house,
Living in sweet cookie-land I won't grouse.
Now my dog wants one built out of kibbles…
Tis better than reality's slaughterhouse.**

VIII

Sip from a jug of laughter to survive,
Self-deprecating words keep us alive.
To stay limber, grin like a yogi, then
laugh at your fate—and you'll be revived.

This Epicurean Pig Seizes the Day With A Nap

Honoring and Remembering Others

As the seasons change, Judy and I take time to remember and honor others. We pay homage to those in the present for making incredible sacrifices and contributions. Others are recollected for having enriched our lives in the past.

In 1954 At Age 6, I Ponder And Recollect.

A Quatrain for Bryan Stevenson

This quatrain honors the leader of the Equal Justice Initiative in Montgomery, Alabama. Bryan Stevenson has dedicated his life to serving the poor, incarcerated and condemned. In *Just Mercy* he writes powerfully about his quest and the people he counseled as a lawyer and friend.

Author of Just Mercy

XXII

How many lies can one soul unmask?
Seeking justice, you didn't have to ask.
Counseling poor, abused and broken folk.
You've filled us with mercy—tis no small task!

A Quatrain for Amy Krouse Rosenthal

The next poem is dedicated to the lively spirit of Amy Krouse Rosenthal. Her children's books were beloved by many families. Amy's thoughtful and original 2007 memoir *Encyclopedia of an Ordinary Life* was very popular and is still requested in bookstores today.

Her final essay was entitled *You May Want to Marry My Husband.* In this piece she wrote a dating profile for him, knowing she did not have long to live. It was a love letter, a good-bye, and an attempt to help Jason Rosenthal get started on the next chapter of his life. Ovarian cancer would claim her life 10 days later in March of 2017.

XCVI

Child pushes elevator button and smiles.
The moon appears to rise at noon meanwhile.
Amy finds comic-drama in small details.
Insightful laughter filled in her profile.

Jacks Eulogy

My Last Ride With Jack

*Here we sit atop Tumwater Hill
with Mount Rainier in the background*

He was everything I ever wanted in a dog:
- White and fluffy
- Devoted and playful

Jack's Eulogy

Everyone wanted to touch Jack the dog,
Everyone said how cute he was...
But his fear kept him at a distance...

Tossed about by life's abuse...
As a young pup he became timid and barky
Trying to scare away the boogie men
He could not see...but only sense.

Not many knew that Jack had a tender and gentle soul.
Not many knew he was so very affectionate.

He was peerless.
He brought miles of smiles
to me and judy

Tethered to my heart
with so many melodies.

Now like water
He slips through my hands
To the oceans beyond

And the oceans
streak my face.
Good-bye

DOUBTING RELIGION AND ENDLESS STUDY

Time Waits For No Dog

Khayyám and FitzGerald were life-long skeptics. They questioned the conventional thinking of their days, sometimes at great risk. Though I subscribe to both the realms of science and spirituality, I am very skeptical of dogmatic organized religion and rigid scientific schools of thought. I believe the road to truth follows the path of doubt and questioning.

IX

Our religion and science expanded our view,
Yet in the end we undid our species anew.
Our intelligence was a gift poorly applied,
no longer able, our species to renew.

X

Holy men explained an eye for an eye
The sacred robes clothed so many a lie,
Till reason no longer made any sense,
and people stopped asking whence and why.

Kibbles for the Soul

Franky Skeptically Praying

XI

In ignorance I knocked on heaven's door too late,
Took a number, strained to listen, had to wait.
Honey tasting pieties fell from Holy tongues;
Later saved my heart and soul OUTside the gate.

XII

I studied a cosmos born before time....
then easily seduced by Omarian rhyme...
As Darwin's evolution explained so much,
I then saw rainbows in a teardrop—sublime.

XIII

You cannot argue with mystery
nor debate facts with dead history.
Arguing back to the starting point
this talk becomes a shållow luxury.

Who is the Trainer, Who the Trainee
Lloyd and Kurly, circa 1958

XIV

I fell into a word-stuffed well.
Truth from lie I could no longer tell.
Struck dumb by endless studying,
I close my eyes to escape this hell.

LXXXIV

I hear no echo, only flat silence.
I stare, strain and study empty giants.
Could there be nothing out there at all!
Who can tell me why…Not Faith, Not Science….

XV

Even if you feel you have mastered the game,
Time in the end will checkmate you the same,
The path to knowledge begins in doubt—
Drink love from a cup and bliss reclaim .

CVIII

Returned a stranger to my old homestead,
Ignored, but for memory in my head.
Only the heart can take me home again;
Soaring across time, my wings are full spread.

EPICUREAN FATALISM

Lois and Sandos Carpe Diem

Like the Greek sages, many Eastern philosophers (Buddhist, Taoists, Sikhs, etc.) shun accumulating wealth and worldly goods, status and power, and dependence on individuals. They argue for detachment from power, wealth, or individuals because these blessings come and go at the whim of fate. Thus, many followers believe they can avoid or minimize suffering by living modestly and realizing their attachments are mostly temporary.

While many philosophers and religious leaders use the vocabulary of fatalism, they are still vigorously engaged in their pursuit of truth, freedom, and their beliefs. I discussed the notion of active, engaged, *heroic fatalism* in my earlier title *Sipping From The Rubaiyat's Chalice.* This idea has been delicately introduced in Reinhold Niebuhr's *Serenity Prayer.* He urges us to accept the things we cannot change, seek the courage to change the things we can, and attain the wisdom to know the difference.

XVI

Forget yesterday and tomorrow.
Grasp the present joy, not the sorrow.
Wanting more and more brings emptiness,
Since clocks speak lies—follow wine's arrow.

XVII

Always plan to take leaps of faith,
merrily embrace your many mistakes,
Ever-ready to bail on moonbeam thoughts.
Let go, Move on…Grab a sweet piece of cake.

XVIII

**Never saw a dog turn down a kibble,
Eating dessert FIRST makes life livable.
Sniffing the past, ignoring the future…
Accepting this moment without quibble.**

Franky Chews on My Shoes—Without a Quibble

XIX

**Do you journey long to NO-where,
or puzzle your path to SOME-where?
As footsteps tramp towards our sunset,
we cannot try to know or care.**

XX

**Mystic clouds enchant brain AND heart.
Begin your heroic dream. Just start!
Leaving reason and facts to slumber…
Try always to live your life as art.**

XXI

**We can never grasp the mystery entire.
What is certain, we live and then expire.
Praise not the fool's riddles, nor the many rules,
Rather, grasp a jug, flower, and love's fire.**

Kibbles for the Soul

Literally Grasping an Opportunity

CXV

**Don't repent, they can't hear you after death.
Spend all that you can, before your last breath!
The past was used, the future beyond reach—
Drain your cup until nothing is left.**

C

**As fate pens your part on a hidden page,
fiercely play your brief scene upon the stage.
Pause in the wings and you've waited too long,
In the final act you exit downstage…**

I was unexpectedly cast in Much Ado About Nothing *in high school. After finding it fun, I enjoyed following footlight possibilities across my life.*

TOPICAL POEMS

Franky Splayed

These poems were crafted out of current events. They are often fueled by the headlines describing heroic and villainous acts. I laugh, weep, celebrate, and seek out threads of hope. Sometimes it is exhausting and I fall splayed onto the pillows like Franky. My job is to ponder, write, note, and then move on.

Post Truth Politics

Entering a new Dark Age

XXIII

**The population bomb burst so very distinct,
Climate change, mushroom cloud—can't act or think,
Donald Trump-ed our bets on the future...
Homo Sapiens on sale— since going extinct.**

XXIV

**Druggists asks me to empty my purse,
Their bottomless greed I scream, I curse.
Legalized ROBBERY winks back at me.
Pretending to care seems so perverse.**

Jack in Recovery

XXV

Every great culture always find the vein.
After peaking, Chooses suicide again…
Evangelic Racists push on the Sisyphus rock,
Devoured in Klan's burning cross—empire slain.

CIX

How has evil triumphed over our bliss?
How can we make meaning out of this?
No reason appears before my mind,
Perchance the failure of our double helix.

CXVI

I'm placing long-odds in this messy race—
preferring to raise my voice in this foul place.
Might lose my money, friends, and status…
The silent alternative I can't face.

In Praise of Local Activism

In support of Olympia's Norma Rae's Resistance

XXVI

**It was time to remove the gloves from their fists,
Harnessing their common strength to persist.
Together we'll end his pussy-grabbing jokes,
wiping the childish smirk from his spoiled lips.**

XCIX

**Hold the utopian eccentrics close
breathe in the warm light of the dreamer's prose.
Tyrants try to stifle hopes and ideals…
Dreams stop darkness as fear is deposed.**

Tyrants Fear Dreamers

CXII

From Moscow to Tiananmen Square,
In DC and Paris we were there...
Building a world out of curses and dreams!
Then plutocrats trapped souls in candied snares.

Kibbles for the Soul

Apocalyptic Musings

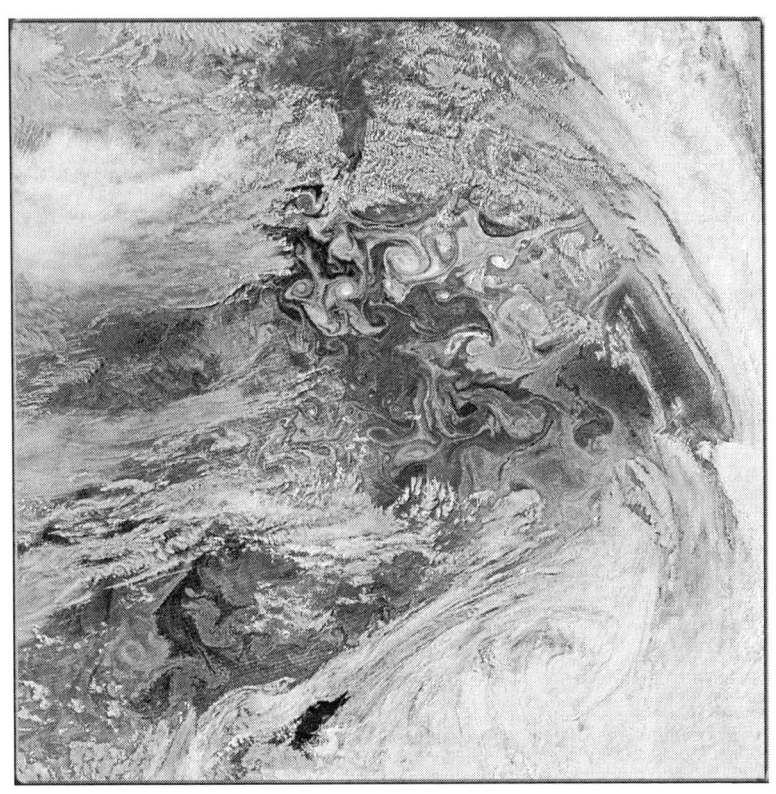

Satellite View of Climate Change

XXVII

Gripping Bible, Torah, Quran—clenched fists and more,
Our world dances on the brink of nuclear war.
Humans cloak their solar system in darkness.
Would aliens come to visit… What for?

LXXXI

Did humans lose a bet with aliens?
They visit, yet stay subterranean.
Our bloody stories proclaim us poorly.
"No more visiting these mammalians."

Pooch Café by cartoonist Paul Gilligan

CIII

Hunting-gathering defined our species,
still waging war and signing treaties.
What have we gathered across these eons?
With a crooked smile, God asks, "Whose are these?"

CXVIII

They're turning abandoned missile silos
into lavish apocalyptic condos.
Condemned to solitary confinement…
Survival of the fittest--bravo!

Kibbles for the Soul

Franky, What me worry?

XXVIII

Heaven weeps and falls from the sky—all too soon.
We'll never carry our sad story beyond the Moon.
God stop this blood-soaked race from poisoning the stars—
The cosmos looks away, our existence impugned.

Kibbles for the Soul

Digital Conundrums

Jack Gets TV On-Demand

What would the FitzOmar "indie" poets write about Facebook , Instagram, robotics and so-called *artificial* intelligence in our digital age?

I agree with philosopher Roman Krznaric that too many people now experience daily life vicariously through the small screen in their hand. He emphatically states that the message in the *Rubáiyát of Omar Khayyám* could bring us back to valuing direct experience in the present moment. As Krznaric notes in his book *Carpe Diem: Seizing the Day in a Distracted World*, we should keep a copy of <u>both</u> the *Rubáiyát* and our iPhone in our pockets. Then, as we absorb the lessons of the FitzOmar team we can hopefully migrate away from the role of observer of life and seize the day as participants.

XXIX

I won't yield to a demographic,
won't surrender to analytics.
The little screen tries to chain my head
to likes, trends, rankings and graphics.

XXX

The stove just informed AmazonFBI
grabbing my data in the blink of an eye.
Why submit to uncaring digi-gods?
Smart appliances record the lie.

Kibbles for the Soul

Cat-a-Tonic Stare

XXXI

**Passwords locked me out in the cold
protecting me from evil I'm told.
Corporate thieves record my every move,
my stolen data so quickly sold.**

XXXII
Thinking machines show evidence
that they exist at our expense.
Smart computers won't need tech support!
I don't believe in Machine-intelligence.

Brave New Digi-World

LXXXV

Dire warnings about password bushwhacks!
My brainwaves…future-thieves plan to highjack!
Fearing artificial intelligence?
I laugh and keep drinking my coffee black.

XXXIII

We seize the Internet of Things—so brave,
riding the over-hyped digital wave.
Elders broadcast vital signs to their docs,
while cursing the Net down into the grave.

Kibbles for the Soul

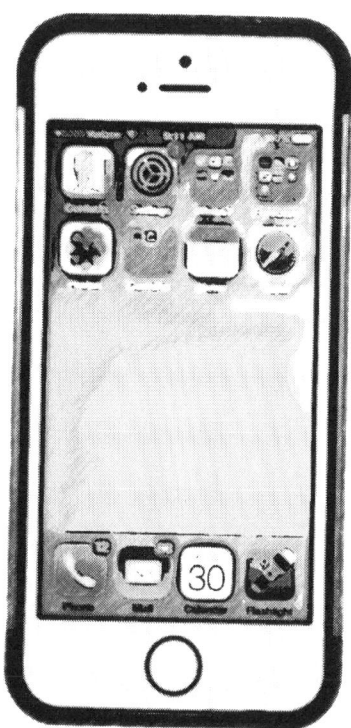

Screened Universe

XCIV

**It had gone too far, the craving complete:
FacebookTwitter endless addicting treat!
Your eyes imprisoned on the tiny screen,
Will you awake from this digital sleep?**

Tool Making Species

CIV

**Tool-making species crafted love and fire;
with Venus and Sisyphus we did conspire.
Promising holy suicide for escape,
Our gifts now heaven's greatest satire.**

HOWLING IN CHANGING TIMES

How do we cope with change? How do we endure, press on? Many of my artistic and political heroes reached great heights, but once their empty cup overfilled, their journeys became conflicted. Many developed exaggerated personality traits that distorted their extraordinary gifts. We never really know the legacy we'll leave behind. We howl in the moment and order catnip for everyone.

Catnip for Everyone

Kibbles for the Soul

Darkness, My Old Friend

CV

**Our cosmos is filled with dark emptiness.
Our final test: the void's mute godlessness.
Pour your song, poem, and drink into the glass,
and find your way into love's warming caress.**

CXIII

The Spirit is spirit, all else just dirt.
Time seems endless, until we grow alert.
Inhale schemes and dreams to sail far beyond...
After blowing away we feel no hurt.

CXIV

Those who have been loved don't want to die.
And still many heads sprout a tearful eye.
Eventually you learn to accept what
providence bestows in your bye-and-bye.

Franky gives us his thoughtful eye

Martini toast to the fallen Camellia

XXXIV

**Ah' the Camellia blooming in early Spring
falls to the ground a beautiful, lonely thing.
The color fades, the blooms blow away,
bravely leaving no imprint …forever unseen.**

Kibbles for the Soul

Singing Them Royal FitzOmar Blues

Quatrain xxxv was inspired by the soulful bulldog lyrics in John Hiatt's song *Face of God*.

Bulldog Wisdom

XXXV

**Sometimes God be the Devil, leaving me to cry,
How much suffering does he want me to try?
They say the tears will cleanse my heart.
When will I be able to look him in the eye?**

Blues Harp Me

XXXVI

Behind the wheel I wailed my blues!
Out of tune I spread the good news.
Blowing my blues harp mostly alone,
this I must Play, my soul to Amuse.

Toasting the Day

I always enjoy raising the glass to reflect.

Toasting the Light

XXXVII

My cocktail glass holds ice and sunbeams,
With my friends I toast unrealistic dreams.
And when I return to dirt, to grow more grape,
Fill a new cup so I can swim in new streams.

XXXVIII

Sharing a drink fractures all my restraint,
my varying reputation it taints.
Happy or sad, we're lost alike in talk.
Remembered as spoiled, dutiful, or saint?

XXXIX

Our conflicted figures come and go,
Apocalypse approaches, this we know.
We must drink, until drunk with ardent love,
before the sky fills with nuclear glow.

XL

Betwixt yesterday and tomorrow
drink now to both your joys and sorrows.
Not knowing when fate beckons you beyond,
toast the endings we cannot know.

XCVII

Too quickly we spill from day into night.
What came before, what comes after...What might?
Briefly enjoy the cup of sweet, sweet life,
Empty the glass and toast being finite.

Emptying the glass to toast being finite

LXXVII

Upon grass I count stars—sparkling carefree,
mumbling numbers I cannot keep, I must agree:
The earth will keep spinning after I go
as sky diamonds keep twinkling without me…

Stars Keep Twinkling
A composite of NASA images

Play2Work2Play

Franky Ceaselessly Playing For Kibbles

In my early adult life I studied and wrote about the search for work and career change. I designed career portfolios as replacements for resumes. Personal

Portfolios were seen as a blend of journaling and scrapbooking. Then at midlife in the 1990s I reflected upon my writer's workaholism. It was a conundrum since my writing was play and work and more play—a necessary ingredient in my life.

I found truth in the Irish playwright George Bernard Shaw's *FitzOmar* lines: *We do not stop playing because we grow old, we grow old when we stop playing.* According to leisure wellness author Forrest McDowell, Plato asserted, "You learn more about a person in an hour of play than a lifetime of conversation." It is during play that we first discover our interests and aptitudes.

These quatrains followed thumbing some of my old titles like, *Portfolio Power* and *Serious Play*.

About Work

XLI

I sat interrogated like a spy,
Telling my story, my endless lies.
Job interviewing is just a blind date,
the truth wills out, after the offer flies.

XLII

The artist's work is absorbed in play,
But for wage-earners there's hell to pay.
Neither should trade an hour of fun
for just one more lost overtime day.

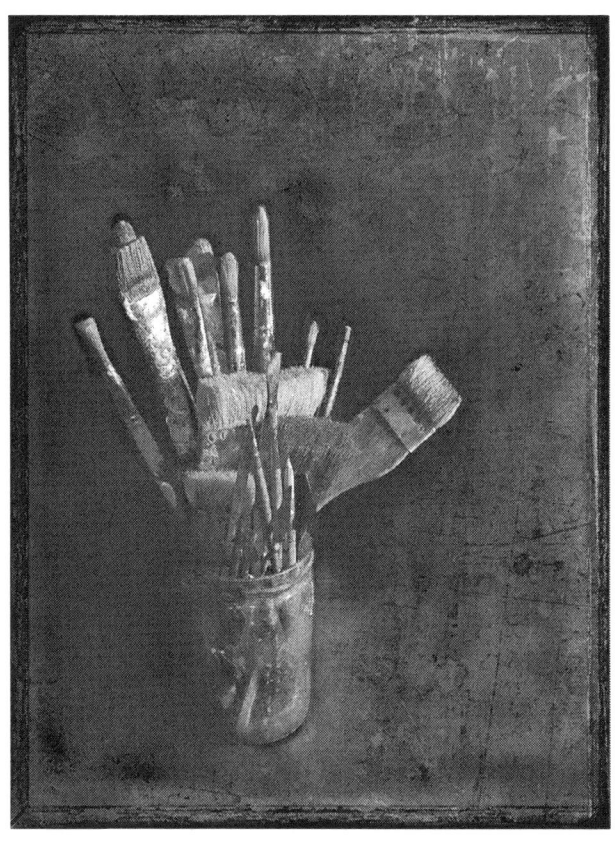

When the Work is Done

XLIII

Fate molds us in an alchemy of tears-n-love,
made from half you and half the stars above;
We shape it only with libation and time.
What purpose lies in these labors of love?

XLIV

Can you relax and toss moments away?
Time is never money when you play.
Do you work to live, or live to work?
Without leisure's rewards, we decay.

About Play

XLV

**The clock is just a ticking machine,
The real timekeeper is a human being.
The twenty-four hours are not all equal.
Leisure's the treasure—work turns obscene.**

XLVI

**Take a vacation from information,
unsubscribe from all notifications,
log out, turn off, dial into deep quiet….
Restore yourself—enjoy the elation.**

Kibbles for the Soul

Franky Practices Doing Nothing

XLVII

**Everyone's smart device sweetly chimes
Everyone has a watch but not the time.
Poor or rich can't stall the draining sands,
Sip ever slowly from forgetful wine.**

XLVIII

**Multi-taskers race clocks like fools
addicted to fast forwarding tools...
Learn the art of doing nothing,
delight within leisure's hidden rules.**

Jack and Judy Playing Nice

XLIX

**If we stop playing, age comes fast and cold
unconsciously trading young for old.
We weep for time so quickly passing,
Slowing down turns free time into gold.**

The Life-Long Career Questions

Hugo Likes To Dress for Success…Next He Must Define It.

Many young people ask, near graduation, "What do I want to do when I grow up?" Then later as they approach retirement they return to a form of the question, "What do I want to do, *now* that I'm grown up?" Thus the question can span a lifetime. In *Gourmet*

Aging I wrote about expanding the word *career* to include an entire lifespan and all the work you perform. For me that includes labors of necessity and labors of love: working for ourselves and serving others.

I urged readers to view retirement as an important time for evaluating their entry into what I called a *second career*. In that book I provided numerous inventories to help readers explore their total career interests across the many domains of paid work, unpaid forms of *work* (volunteering, self-study, schooling, learning), serious play (the art of doing nothing, humor, playfulness, hobbies), and soul work or the pursuit of spiritual issues.

Kibbles for the Soul

What Could I Be Doing Next?

In the Spring of 2017 Lindsay McCoy was facing what she called a quarter-life crisis at age 25. She had worked as a model, teacher and student.

Lindsay is a funny, talented craftsperson, and creative writer—and was a bit lost in that moment. She asked,

"What could I be doing next? I don't want to waste my time or opportunity."

She came over for lunch and we talked. I suggested that we might explore her answers through the medium of her favorite activities writing and modeling. Out of that interaction I ended up writing the following quatrains and then crafted a script for a photo shoot based on some of the themes in these poems.

LXXXVI

Uncertain the journey when you don't know where,
Strike out—any road can get you there!
Life happens while busy making plans,
Wear a face-mask showing us that you care.

LXXXVII

In our youth we must take our greatest dare
There is always time to regroup, repair.
Failing forward is sometimes the only way
to live a life without regrets or despair

LXXXVIII

She did not know what to be at twenty-five.
She was confounded by turning forty-five.
At sixty she asked "What next could I be?"
growing up seems to take an eternity...

LXXXIX

"And what do you do, can I have your card?"
You're not a job title—an old canard.
Retirement turns your story on its head,
so hand them lyrics on our leisure card

Kibbles for the Soul

Which Path Will Jack Take?

XC

**Chance, hard work brings me to foothills of fame.
Could the summit be calling me by name?
Others with less talent look down upon me.
When is it enough…in this wondering game?**

XCI

What does success look like when it's your turn?
Do you fantasize about what you'd earn?
Does your real triumph elude your gaze,
blinded by the golden sun you yearn.

XCVIII

Wine sipped from the cup is forever changed,
Nothing in this world ever remains the same.
Wealth and status fluctuate with the winds,
Learn what's most valuable, and life reclaim.

CELEBRATING LOVE

Tea Time for Judy and Mitzi

People have asked why I write so much. To paraphrase Steinbeck, they may as well ask why I breathe so much. I understand my world only when I write, photograph, create and dream onwards. Maybe this partially explains why I've written love poems to Judy for over 40 years.

Kibbles for the Soul

Love Notes and Poems for Judy

Every year I write my Judy three poems. In 2016 I decided that all future poems to her would take the form of FitzOmarDorf quatrains. The next year's poems were completed before I had to unexpectedly go into the hospital after falling.

The day before my surgery Omar tapped me on the forehead. He suggested that I deliver the poems before I go in for a shoulder joint replacement. This is from the letter I wrote Judy the day before…

> *My Dear, Dear Judy,*
>
> *I send this to you before I go in to the hospital. At our advanced age all surgery comes with a risk as much as a promise.*
>
> *I promise to always love you forever, and slightly beyond. I am expecting to see you when I awake and if that is not an option I want to share my final quatrains with you.*
>
> *These are the three quatrains for 2017. You can wait to read them with me in person and if that is not a choice then read these small poems and toast me with a scotch and soda…*

Valentine's Day, February 14

L

Where is Cupid, he has broken my heart?
Why has he left me a world both cold and dark!
Toss the peanuts and bring me a stiff drink...
Amidst stupid ones, loving you keeps me smart

Valentine's Day Smooch

Judy's Birthday, February 23

LI

**The world has become a broiling roiling mess
I have lost my hope I must confess.
I see bits of light upon the crown of your head
Maybe in your birthday cake I can find a YES**

Our 41st anniversary, August 5

LII

**Did you ever think we would break 40?
A hall of fame can hold no greater glory.
Time has flown on laughing wings of love,
as we author more scenes in our story…**

Love Me Anytime (written after recuperation…)

Love Scratches My Itch

LIII

**Your healing heart so big—completes myself,
so generous your love, in and of itself.
Teaching me how to laugh away the blues,
can't finish this journey with anyone else.**

For J's 2018 valentine

LXXVIII

The mingling spirits have always been ours;
while infinite gestures are held by the stars,
Your holding my hand reaches far beyond,
your velvet touch opens to our boudoir.

For J's 2018 birthday

LXXIX

Awakening with grin and bird nest hair
Drawn to morning's window—out you stare.
You'll never become a frail old lady…
while listing to-do's in to-day's prayer.

August 5 2018

CXX

Once YWCA, now LRS President.
Taking charge, pinned into your firmament!
At home you're the CEO of our dreams.
I adore your gifted management.

Forever

CI

Arm in arm we stroll memory's golden fields.
Heart to heart we kiss, meld, and gently yield,
Talking, sipping, eating, teasing, laughing...
Pains falls before pleasures, and all is healed.

THE PARADOXES IN OUR AGING

Jack Joins Me On My Father's Memorial Pilgrimage

Ah! The joke may be on us, otherwise why else would youth be wasted on the young. These poems explore the pluses and minuses bestowed upon us as we grow older. And if we remain curiously learning and adjust to what is left, then we also gather unto us a bit of wisdom.

LIV

The silhouettes prance across a canvas screen.
So many truths turn out not what they seem.
Youth's aimless image floats quickly by…
Once gone, our song joins the ancient scream.

LV

Was my story of youth a useful lie?
Words shouted before a darkening sky!
Trading my vigor for wisdom's folly,
Life's grin stolen with a kiss good-bye.

LVI

Before the timer stops and is due
write a story both false and true.
While you cannot edit your real life
Try drafting an obit that works for you.

LVII

My obit writ with humor and lies,
as mortality releases my final ties.
I may get there before you do,
Tis never really a final good-bye.

LVIII

With age comes pain and a final test.
I hear the Earth calling, "It's time for a rest!"
Longevity is highly over-rated.
Quickly going home tis probably best.

Franky Travels in His Mind

LIX

As we add years we gather pain,
subtraction is the aging game,
Life's thorny muse feeds us wisdom
as infinite sleep calls our name…

LX

We first learn to crawl then slow-walk-chained.
Growing old deducts from body and brain.
The farthest we travel is in our mind,
Ending at the edge of our mortal plane.

LXI

Don't give me your medical report,
I just want to hear what you still ache for...
Holding my hand, gaze into my eyes;
My greatest pain is a life tooo short.

CXIX

When young, time shimmers towards the infinite,
Later it galloped—and I could not slow it…
Einstein taught how the clock is relative.
Time won't fit life, so make the most of it.

Kibbles for the Soul

Pondering Life's Transience

LXII

Gimme one more sip from my pink martini,
One more time to ski the slopes, unruly.
My Life unfolds—an improbable joke…
Laughing then cleansing with tears unduly.

LXIII

Sipping martinis on my final slide
yelling, "WahHoo what a terrific ride!!"
Kindly help pull the plugs and tubes away!!
Breaking rules as I slide out with the tide...

Ageless On Two Wheels

CHASING LIFE'S SHADOW SHOW

Franky's Sketchy Look

Why we come and why we go, we simply don't know. Our stories are blended from fate, effort, luck—set before a cosmic laugh. At times, it feels like we are props in a shadow show.

LXIV

Randomly around the sphere we come and go
Nothing is promised but death, that we know.
We come unbidden, and after Dark descends
we utter, " I now know something you don't know."

Martin, Jack and Cigar—What Do They Know?

LXV

Why have I come and given great chase?
How does it end, was it all a waste?
Can Not asking lead to More knowing?
Soon my passing feeds another's haste.

LXVI

Staring along the horizon, making big plans,
Stars laugh—Our designs twisting in their hands.
Our hopes and goals fuel heaven's laughter.
Stop to sip wine, before crossing shifting sands.

CVII

Bob went to war; came home to drive a bus.
He liked to bowl, fish and play jokes on us...
His obit left the faintest trace behind,
And now his story's lost in timelessness.....

Kibbles for the Soul

Franky Staring At The Horizon

LXVII

**Sunlight tries to bathe us in our womb,
then moonlight descends upon fallen blooms.
The vineyard grows ever so sweet, as my
memory's swept clean by history's broom.**

Bailey Looking for Another Glass…

LXVIII

**Death's door opens on the greatest fear,
could we reincarnate to find nothing here?
Avoid spending precious time in despair,
Sip deep and accept your image in the mirror.**

XCII

Asleep we soared on bright butterfly wings.
Was I dramatizing her insect schemes
or she naively performing in mine?
Does birth or death awake us from the dream?

Franky Dreaming Eyes Open

XCIII

When we fall into the endless sleep
are we only restored when others weep,
or do we awake in another form?
Is it the fragments or the whole we keep?

THE STAR DUSTY SKY

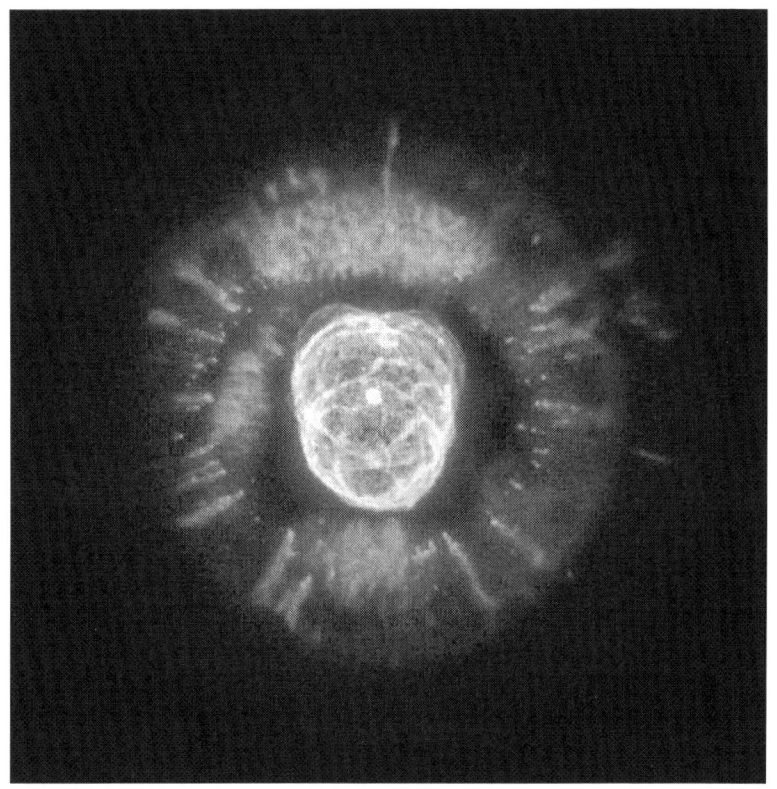

Eskimo Nebula

Credit NASA/Andrew Fruchter (STScI)

On my birthday in 2017, the Danspace Instagram feed contained a reposting of his Eskimo Nebula blog. The nebula (known as NGC 2392) was originally found by Frederick William Herschel on January 17, 1787. The remnant light of this now-gone nebula remind one of an Eskimo's face surrounded by a winter parka hood.

His reflections are entitled *Out of Time*. It was one of the most poetic and thoughtful cosmological essays I have ever read. Dan's musings inspired these quatrains. The original post can be found on his blog if you type *https://danspace77.com* into your Google search box.

LXIX

Hubble Telescope sends us across time and space
revealing an ancient supernova face.
Did they temper instincts in order to survive?
Will others look back at our Milky Way with grace?

LXX

Eskimo Star-dwellers flew on astral sails.
hesitant to follow stardusty trails…
What choices were made back in deep space? Or
were they just shadows in a cosmic folktale?

LXXI

Will our species endure its self-inflicted folly,
to rub noses with the Eskimo finale?
Or did we only crawl from dinosaur swamps,
to be consumed by silent melancholy?

Franky Wonders About His Destiny

LXXXII

The moon—our tranquil and silent partner,
We howl at it and often wonder…
No matter our complaint or our boast
Luna remains a patient listener.

LXXII

Our tale unwinds oddly and briefly.
No one knows our final destiny—
Returning to the larger cosmic code,
no longer bound by our mortality…

DRAINING THE CUP

*The Kibble Soul Brothers
Bid Good-Bye*

CII

**April third in I turned GodDamn 70.
But my genetics said this would not be,
My expiration date was 65…
I guess the cosmic joke was played on me!**

LXXIII

Why does the word Mortality
rhyme so easily with Fatality?
Skipping and dancing with Duality…
In the end whispering Finality.

LXXIV

My Meter is not always kept the same.
I write in the spirit of play and game.
Don't mine my poems like hard lumps of coal, Instead
let verse stir ashes back into flame.

LXXV

Writing hands sum up my journey in this book.
Age, arthritis bequeath a tempered outlook.
Come sip from the Rubáiyát's Chalice,
and reflect upon gourmet meals left to cook.

Kibbles for the Soul

Franky Sails Across The Checkerboard

CVII

Firmly make your move within the flow.
The edge of the board comes quickly... you know.
The checkerboard has no in-between grays—
We come, travel quickly...then must go.

Kibbles for the Soul

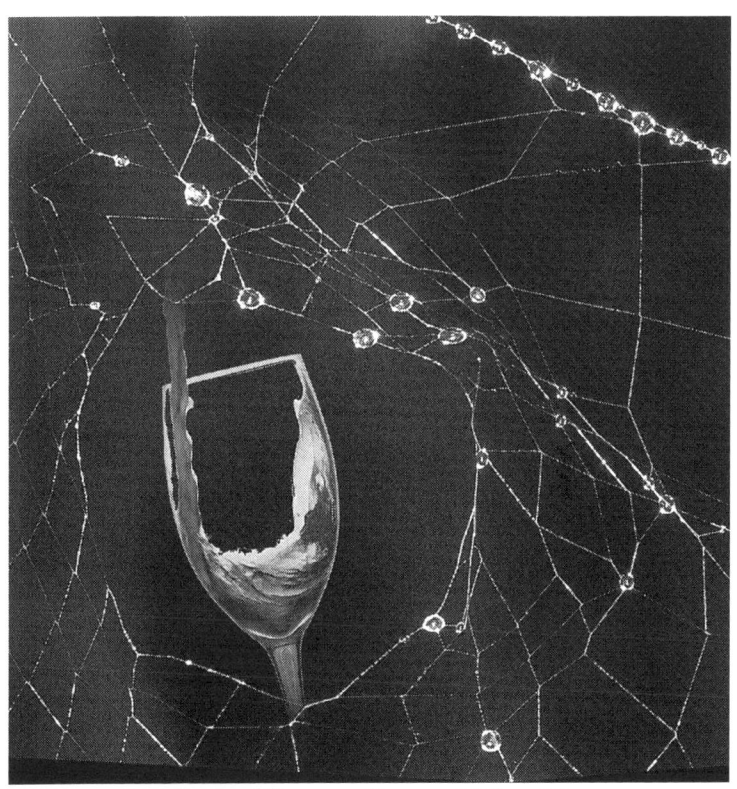

Some Glimpse Beyond The Glass

CXI

Flitting like bugs in an alien's jar,
not understanding who we really are.
Some glimpse beyond the glass, most remain blind…
The pest persists—a trivial commissar.

Kibbles for the Soul

Clouded Time

CVI

**Let's speak of the once that was yesterday...
Stories recalled from the gold leaf dossier.
Ignore tomorrow's beckoning finger,
the ringing phone, ticking clock—we disobey**

LXXVI

**Blissfully cooking a gourmet meal one more time,
my life spent searching for fate's plan and rhyme.
Drained the cup; turned it over without regret…
recalling friends and drink, in love entwined.**

Drain the Cup and Think of Me

Artwork and Acknowledgements

Martin Kimeldorf created or developed most of the artwork and photomontages from front to back covers. This includes interpreting and collaging images found in the cosmology images found in the public domain at the NASA web site, pictures restored from old family albums and *Kibble Soul Brothers* shot by his brother Lloyd.

The cartoons and photos are reprinted here with permission. This includes Pooch Café cartoons by Paul Gilligan; the picture of *Hugo the Dog* by Marko Savkovich; Irine Parini's two images *Cat-a-Tonic Stare* and *Darkness, My Old Friend*; and Julie Wagners spider web in *Some Glimpse Beyond The Glass*.

Editorial contributions and encouragements from my wife Judy and brother Howard helped get this work off and running. Reassuring comments from FitzOmar experts Bill Martin, Sandra Mason, and Bob Richardson paved the way for completing this project. This was followed by positive and helpful feedback from Lois Talotta, Jacque Hudlow, Karen Upton. Then there was Alison Keithley; she was my pivotal reviewer in the beginning and finisher at the end. Thank you all for keeping me company on this journey.

My Other Essays and Books You Might Enjoy

On my ancient and unkempt website you can find these two the **free essays**. Go to www.martinkimeldorf.org and then click on the Soul Work page for these two items:

Cosmic Coding

Light and Shadow

Recent **books in print and eBook** formats include:

Writing An Obituary Worth Reading
A Guide to Writing a Fulfilling Life-Review

My Mixology
Cocktails, Funny Tales & Literary Sleight of Hand

How To Stay In Love, Forever
...Forty-plus Years of Love Poems, Letters, and PhotoArt

Sipping From The Rubáiyát's Chalice
My Journey with The Rubáiyát of Omar Khayyám

Made in the USA
San Bernardino, CA
31 August 2017